Job Power

Master the Job Search

by Jurg Oppliger

illustrated by Mike Gorman

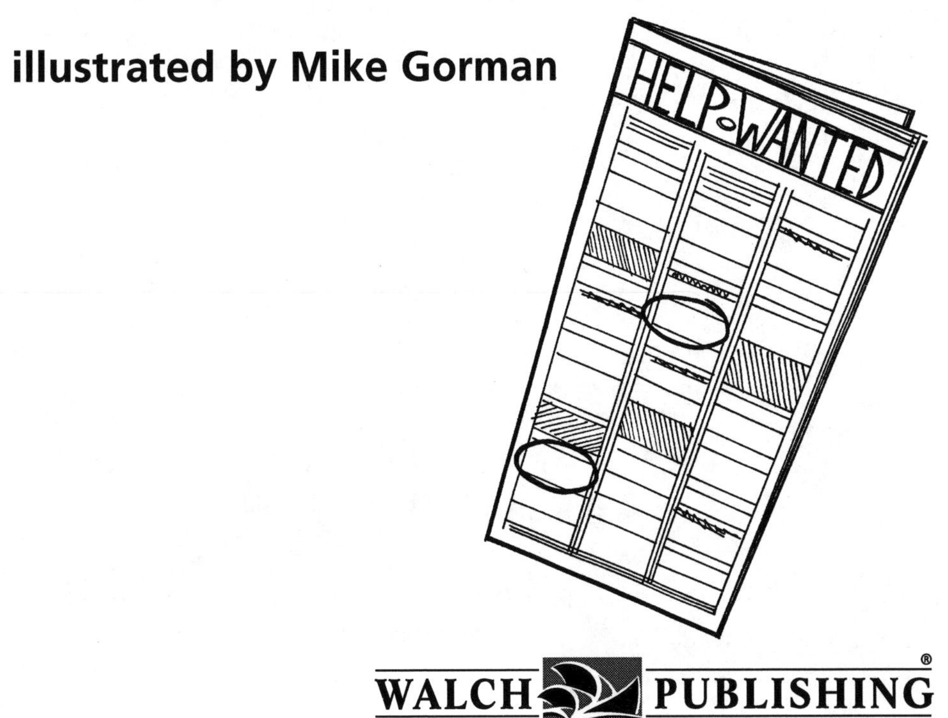

WALCH PUBLISHING®

I would like to thank
my wife Barbara
for her moral support
and her proofreading.

2 3 4 5 6 7 8 9 10
ISBN 0-8251-3821-3

J. Weston Walch, Publisher
P [illegible]

Distributed By:
Grass Roots Press
Toll Free: 1-888-303-3213
Fax: (780) 413-6582
Web Site: www.grassrootsbooks.net

Contents

Preparing for the Job Search

You are planning one of the most important steps in your life: looking for a full-time job. You wonder what your chances of finding a good job are.

If you go about your job search in the right way, your chances are much better than you think. Every day, many thousands of men and women find a job in the United States. Every day, thousands of men and women start in a new workplace. This book will help you become one of them.

This is not a book to read, this is a **Work Book,** a how-to kit. In it I will help you write a good résumé, and show you how to use it for each of the four proven ways to find a job.

Action sheets are for you to write in. You will fill them in with your ideas, conclusions, and drafts. You will find that writing helps you develop clear, well-formulated ideas.

To get started, read quickly through the whole book. This will tell you what to expect. Then go through it in detail, filling in all the action sheets.

I was a top manager in two very different industries, and personally hired a lot of men and women, managers, office workers, and manual workers. I organized some takeovers and mergers, and had to let a number of employees go. Realizing the problems these people faced, I left my job and started a career transition company. In the last 10 years I have helped hundreds of men and women decide what kind of a job they should be looking for, and have shown them how to find it. This book is the outcome of my experience. It will not try to psychoanalyze you or teach you any fancy theories. It will just teach you how to master the job search process.

PART 1

Laying the Groundwork

Before you start looking for a job, you should know what kind of job you want. If you're not sure about this, you're not really ready to begin the job search yet. You should be able to describe your ideal job. That way, you will be able to decide whether or not a particular job is right for you.

As soon as you have that ideal job description, you need to start making lists of places that might need someone like you, and a list of people you can contact to talk about work. You should also study the Help Wanted ads in the local newpaper and cut out any ads that look interesting. Don't answer the ads for the time being, just keep them. You may want to answer them when you have worked your way through this book.

Action Sheet 1: The Ideal Job

The Company

Location

First priority: __________
Other acceptable areas: __________
Acceptable commuting distance: __________

Kind of Company

Big corporation or small company? __________
Local, national, worldwide? __________

Type of Industry

Manufacturing? Trading? Service? Government? __________

Company Culture

Management style, structure, etc: __________
Kind of direct superior: __________
What kind of person do I work best with? __________

My Job

My Activity

Accounting, administration, data processing, manufacturing, selling, other:

____

My Level of Responsibility

Assistant to somebody, clerical job, shop floor worker, supervisor, other:

____

Working Hours

Shift worked: __________
Days worked: __________

Compensation

I want to earn $ ______________________________
I need to earn at least $ ______________________________
I am/am not willing to have part of my pay as commission or bonus.

____

Benefits

List employee benefits that are important for you to have.

1. ______________________________
2. ______________________________
3. ______________________________
4. ______________________________
5. ______________________________
6. ______________________________
7. ______________________________
8. ______________________________
9. ______________________________
10. ______________________________

The Company

Using the criteria you identified above, and any other thoughts you have, describe the ideal company.

____
____
____
____
____

My Job

Using the criteria you identified above, and any other thoughts you have, describe your ideal job.

____
____
____
____

Your Target List

A list of possible employers will be your Target List. Start by listing any employers you already know who match your focus. Develop a list of key words that describe the target industry. For example, if your ideal job was working as a cook, you might list:

- restaurants
- diners
- resorts
- retail food service
- corporate food service
- hotels

Your Key Words:

____

____

____

____

____

Use these key words to find employers to add to your Target List. If you worked before, think about competitors, customers, suppliers, or other companies in the same field. Look in the Yellow Pages, using your key words. Read the business section of the newspaper. Whenever you see a company that may be of interest, add it to your Target List.

Sample Document 1: Target List

Company Name	Contact	Remarks
Private Practice Institute	*Amy Laughlin, events coordinator*	*organize and present workshops around the country*
Decorous Decor	*Jorge Diaz*	*small import firm*
Odd Man Out		*Retail—toys and games*

Action Sheet 2: Your Target List

Company Name	Contact	Remarks

Your Networking List

The other list that you will need to start now is a list of contacts—your Networking List. Networking is simply talking to people. Your networking list will include names of people you can talk to. These people do not need to be friends, or even acquaintances. They just need to be people you have enough of a connection with to start a conversation. If you can pick up the phone and call them, for any reason, they are possible networking contacts.

Start your Networking List with the names of personal contacts: family, friends, acquaintances, classmates, teachers, club members. Then list professional contacts: employers, supervisors, colleagues, customers.

For each person, write the person's name, telephone number, and any information that you think might be helpful—the name of the person who introduced you, the names of the contact's children, and so forth. As you work through this book, keep adding to your list of contacts. You will see how to use it later on.

Sample Document 2: Networking List

Name	Phone (home/office)	Remarks
Jim Buzzell	*home 987-6543*	*Wife Heidi, son Peter*
Tom Bardolino	*office 456-7890*	*Rotary, insurance broker*
Bill Warney		*Met at Uncle Joe's*

Action Sheet 3: Your Networking List

Name	Phone (home/office)	Remarks

Success Stories

To gain the self-confidence you need to go out and get a good job, you have to think about past successes, and write about them. We are all measured and judged by our actions, much more than by our words. To have your future employer judge you by your actions, you have to tell him or her about them, about your successes. This chapter prepares you to talk about the things you have done well in the past.

What is a success story? A success can be

- Something you were complimented on—by a teacher, a friend, your boss, or a colleague
- Something that nobody else commented on, but you were proud of
- Something you went home and proudly told your parents and friends about

When you're looking for success stories, don't just look for big things. You may not have had any major successes. But you have certainly had some triumphs and achievements, be it in school, in sports, at work, with your friends or with your family.

In order to keep your success stories short and concise, structure them in three parts:

- the problem, situation, or circumstances
- what you did to change it
- the result of your action

First, describe the problem, the circumstances, or the situation. Try to do it in one sentence. Then write down what you did to change the situation or solve the problem. Finally, in one or two sentences, describe the result. Let me give you an example:

Sample Document 3: Success Stories

Problem: *My math grades were consistently poor.*

Action: *During the summer vacation, despite holding down a summer job, I went through all the math tests from the last semester. I found a colleague strong in math who helped me see where I went wrong. The first day in class I saw my math teacher and told her that I had worked hard and that I wanted to improve my math grades.*

Result: *The teacher was sympathetic and helpful. When I received a good grade on the first test she complimented me in front of the whole class.*

This is a good example with a visible and quantifiable result. Not all successes can be quantified. Try to include as many concrete success stories as you can.

Action Sheet 4: My Success Stories

Write up at least four success stories. If you have more, write them on a separate sheet of paper.

1. **Problem** ____________________

   Action ____________________

   Result ____________________

2. **Problem** ____________________

   Action ____________________

   Result ____________________

3. **Problem** ____________________

   Action ____________________

   Result ____________________

4. **Problem** ____________________

   Action ____________________

   Result ____________________

Action Sheet 5: What Are My Skills?

Through school, work, home, and volunteer activities, we all develop certain skills. These can include very specific skills—able to operate a forklift, able to perform CPR—and more general skills—excellent writing skills, good at math. What are your skills? List at least 10 skills that you have developed.

1. ______________________________

2. ______________________________

3. ______________________________

4. ______________________________

5. ______________________________

6. ______________________________

7. ______________________________

8. ______________________________

9. ______________________________

10. ______________________________

Action Sheet 6: Qualities of Success

Look back at your list of Success Stories. What personal quality helped you succeed in each one? Look at the example of the student with poor math grades. In this case, determination and persistence were probably the keys to success. Other personal qualities include:

- ability to communicate
- direction
- high energy level
- initiative
- interpersonal skills
- self-knowledge
- competitiveness
- flexibility
- imagination
- intelligence
- leadership
- willingness to accept responsibility

List the personal qualities that have helped you succeed here.

PART 2

Create a Winning Résumé

The Purpose of a Résumé

What is a résumé for? You may think, it is meant to get you a job. But nobody I know has ever been hired based on a résumé. Your résumé is one step in the job-finding process, often the first one. When you send out your résumé, you hope it will get picked out of the mass of other résumés and **result in an interview**. Interviews get you a job, not résumés!

The résumé, therefore, has to make you look interesting. It has to leave some questions open that will only be answered in an interview. So, do not give too much information, but make yourself look as good as possible by showing the positive things you did in school or in your last jobs.

In this section, you will see what happens when a company receives your résumé, and will learn how to write a résumé that will get you noticed.

What Happens to Your Résumé?

Imagine for a moment what happens when you answer an ad:

Step 1: The person looking at the incoming offers may have anywhere from 50 to 200 or more letters and résumés to go through. Do you think they read all the résumés? Certainly not! They look at the cover letters (you will learn all you have to know about cover letters in the next chapter), they glance at the résumés, and make two piles: "Possibles" and "Rejects." You get in the "Possibles" pile if your résumé is of a reasonable length and if something of interest can be seen at first glance. That means either the cover letter or the first paragraph of your résumé has to catch this busy person's attention.

In some big companies, nobody will read your résumé. It will be scanned electronically. These Résumé Management Systems will look for key words in your résumé, and will give a "recommendation" to look more closely at your résumé based on how many of the key words specified for the job in question show up in your résumé. That's one reason why it's important to use such key words if you apply to an employment agency or a big company. These key words can be verbs or nouns, and cover professional skills, interpersonal skills, or knowledge.

Step 2: A closer study of the "Possibles" helps decide whom to invite for a first interview. You are selected if you offer some "customer benefits," as the advertising people call it. That means something of particular interest to the company, and **something that not everyone else offers.**

Step 3: The first interview, often with about six candidates, will determine who will be invited for a second interview. In larger companies, the first interview is usually conducted by the Human Resources Department. Only the second interview is conducted by the head of the department that is hiring. In small companies, the department head or owner may get directly involved, and there may even be only one interview.

Step 4: The second interview, normally with two or three candidates. A decision is sometimes made at this stage, but sometimes there is a third (or even a fourth) interview.

Essentials of a Winning Résumé

Since the objective of the résumé is to get you an interview, it must

- have a first paragraph that presents your strengths.
- be short: one or two pages.
- give examples of accomplishments.
- present a picture of you that leaves some questions open.

Types of Résumés

Every résumé is different, because every résumé describes different skills and experience. But all résumés need to give the same basic information. Because of this, most résumés use one of two standard formats: chronological or functional. Even if you are preparing a résumé to be scanned or to download on the Internet, it should still follow a standard format.

Chronological Résumé

The most common résumé is the chronological one. This type of résumé lists all your experience or education in reverse chronological order, the most recent things first, the earlier ones last.

Functional Résumé

This résumé format summarizes your work in terms of "functions," or what you did on the job. It minimizes your employment history. Since employers are used to seeing chronological résumés, you should only choose this format if a chronological résumé does not give a good picture of your background.

Sample Document 4: Chronological Résumé

Darrell Kane
23 Sea Road
Upville, NY 11545
(516) 123-5678
E-mail: skane@upville.net

Summary

A competent, dependable office professional with extensive experience using computers and other office equipment.

Work Experience

1996–1999: U.S. Air Force, Shreveport, LA
Sortie Support Flight Technician

- Loaded data into computers
- Inspected delicate equipment for defects
- Processed detail records for inquiries
- Accountable for $3 million of military hardware
- Supervised night shift with two subordinates

1993–1996: U.S. Air Force, Rome, NY
Crew Chief

- Maintained records of maintenance performed on the aircraft
- Inspected the entire airframe for damage
- Trained as a supervisor for assigned airframe

Other Skills

- Knowledgeable of MS Word, Windows 95, Excel, Lotus, and Prodigy software
- Accurately type 40 wpm
- Familiar with operation of multiline phones, copiers, and fax machines
- Able to communicate orally and in writing
- Skilled at planning and organizing events

Education

Anacortes High School, Seattle, WA
1993: High School Diploma

Sample Document 5: Functional Résumé

Elena Ortiz
23 Main, San Antonio, TX 78245
Tel: (210) 555-5555

Summary

Reliable, computer-literate high school graduate. Good communication and math skills.

Education

1993: Diploma, Santa Anna High School
Courses: Public Speaking, English, Math, Computers

Skills and Abilities

Communication:

- Delivered 45-minute speeches to 160 people in Public Speaking Class
- Taught English teacher to jump-start her 1978 VW Microbus
- Taught woodworking class to 38 kids as camp counselor

Selling

- Sold my car, negotiated with customers, got my asking price
- Persuaded 14 businesses to sponsor ads in high school yearbook
- Generated $467.35 for SADD fund-raiser

Math

- Maintained solid "B" average in all four years of high school
- Computed own 1040EZ tax return, received $340 federal refund
- Constantly use fractions, decimals, percentages in woodworking

Computers

- Proficient in use of IBM and Macintosh computers (high school computer class)
- Assisted uncle in understanding how to operate his new IBM PC
- Enjoy the challenge of learning new programs

Activities

- Play second-string varsity basketball
- Enjoy automobiles and woodworking

The Parts of a Résumé

A good chronological résumé has five parts.

- Your name and address, including phone number and, if you have them, fax number and e-mail address
- A summary (three to six lines) that describes your main strengths
- A summary of your educational background: If you attended various schools or universities, start with the last one. Include any courses or classes you have taken, including in-house training, on-the-job training and summer courses.
- A list of all the jobs you have had, including voluntary work you were not paid for
- Additional information, for example:

  1. Time spent in the Army, Navy, Air Force, Coast Guard
  2. Honors and awards
  3. Successes in sports or clubs and associations
  4. Publications: term papers and articles you wrote
  5. Inventions you made or patents you hold
  6. Membership in associations
  7. A hobby that has a connection with your job

Action Sheet 7: Assembling the Parts

These pages will lead you through the steps of creating a résumé.

Identifying Information

The first information anyone looking at your résumé sees should be the information that identifies you and shows how to contact you.

Name

If you have a nickname, you may need to decide whether to use your given name on the résumé, or the name most people know you by. Imagine that your new employer will have a nameplate and business cards made up for you. What name would you want on your business cards? Use that name on your résumé.

Name: ____

Address

This should be the address where you would like résumé-related correspondence to be mailed. If your home address was in Illinois but you were staying with a friend in Seattle and looking for a job in the Seattle area, you would give your Seattle address on the résumé.

Street Address: ______________________________________

City, State, Zip: ______________________________________

Telephone Number and E-mail

Make sure you give a telephone number where you are sure a message will get through. If an employer can't get through to you to set up an interview, you aren't going to get the job. It's always a good idea to include the area code with the telephone number. You should only include your work number if it is okay for possible employers to call you at work. Include your e-mail address if you check your e-mail regularly.

Home Phone: ____

Work Phone: ____

E-mail: ____

Summary

This section is a brief statement of your experience, training, and personal abilities. It should be very short—three or four sentences at most. Writing a summary can be quite a challenge. As you write, keep the job you want in mind. Think about the skills needed to succeed in that area. Which of these skills have you developed? What personal strengths do you want to highlight? Include them in your summary. If you still find it hard to come up with a good summary, prepare the rest of the résumé first. Some people find it easier to write this section after they have written about their past work experiences. You can come back to this section later.

____

____

____

____

Education

This section is designed to show an employer that you have the education needed to do the job. If you have attended more than one school, start with the most recent one. Each entry should include the name and location of the school, when you graduated, what you studied, any honors or awards you received, and your extracurricular activities.

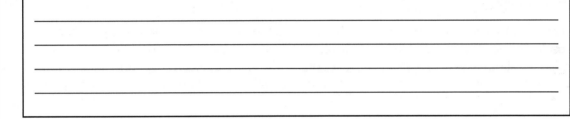

Educational Institution: ______________________

City, State: ______________________

Year of Graduation: __________ Diploma/Degree/Certificate: __________

Major Programs Studied: ______________________

Academic Achievements, Honors, Awards: ______________________

Extracurricular Activities: ______________________

Educational Institution: ______________________

City, State: ______________________

Year of Graduation: __________ Diploma/Degree/Certificate: __________

Major Programs Studied: ______________________

Academic Achievements, Honors, Awards: ______________________

Extracurricular Activities: ______________________

Educational Institution: ____________________
City, State: ____________________
Year of Graduation: __________ Diploma/Degree/Certificate: __________
Major Programs Studied: ____________________
Academic Achievements, Honors, Awards: ____________________
Extracurricular Activities: ____________________

Work Experience

Employers know that the best way to tell what a person *can* do on a job is to see what the person *has* done. This section should tell an employer what you've done at work in the past. Remember, "work" doesn't just mean work you were paid for. If you've worked as a volunteer or as an intern, that experience counts, too. Include it on your résumé. Start with your most recent job. List where you worked, the dates of employment, the position you held, and your duties.

Employer: ____________________ Dates of Employment: __________
Employer's Location (City, State): ____________________
Position Title: ____________________
Job Duties: ____________________
____
____
____

Employer: ____________________ Dates of Employment: __________
Employer's Location (City, State): ____________________
Position Title: ____________________
Job Duties: ____________________
____
____
____

Employer: ______________________ Dates of Employment: __________

Employer's Location (City, State): ______________________

Position Title: ______________________

Job Duties: ______________________

____

____

____

Employer: ______________________ Dates of Employment: __________

Employer's Location (City, State): ______________________

Position Title: ______________________

Job Duties: ______________________

____

____

____

Additional Information

Is there any other important information that doesn't fit into any of the sections above? Have you spent time in the Army, Navy, Air Force, or National Guard? Have you published a book or an article? Have you received an honor or award in your community? Have you invented anything, or do you hold a patent? Are you a member of any associations? Do you have a hobby that relates to the job you want? Do you have computer experience, like programming? Write this additional information here.

____

____

____

____

____

____

____

____

✔ Checklist 1: Action Verbs

When you wrote down the information about what you did in each job, what did you say? Employers aren't interested in what your job required; they want to know what *you* did. The best way to do this is to use action verbs. Instead of saying, "Responsibilities included maintaining cash drawer," try "Reconciled cash drawer at end of shift." Here is a list of some action verbs. Check any that could be used to describe what you did on the job. You will use them for the first draft of your résumé.

____ acquired	____ changed	____ determined
____ acted	____ clarified	____ developed
____ adapted	____ classified	____ devised
____ advised	____ coached	____ diagnosed
____ aided	____ collaborated	____ directed
____ allocated	____ collected	____ distributed
____ analyzed	____ compiled	____ doubled
____ anticipated	____ composed	____ drafted
____ appraised	____ condensed	____ edited
____ arranged	____ constructed	____ eliminated
____ assembled	____ consulted	____ enabled
____ assessed	____ contracted	____ enforced
____ assisted	____ controlled	____ established
____ balanced	____ coordinated	____ evaluated
____ budgeted	____ created	____ examined
____ built	____ cultivated	____ expanded
____ calculated	____ defined	____ explained
____ catalogued	____ demonstrated	____ facilitated
____ centralized	____ designed	____ familiarized

____ formed
____ founded
____ generated
____ guided
____ handled
____ hired
____ identified
____ implemented
____ improved
____ incorporated
____ increased
____ inspected
____ installed
____ instructed
____ integrated
____ interpreted
____ interviewed
____ introduced
____ invented
____ investigated
____ launched
____ maintained
____ managed
____ marketed
____ mediated
____ minimized
____ monitored
____ motivated
____ negotiated
____ observed
____ obtained
____ operated
____ organized
____ originated
____ overhauled
____ oversaw
____ participated
____ performed
____ planned
____ prepared
____ prioritized
____ processed
____ produced
____ programmed
____ projected
____ purchased
____ qualified
____ recommended
____ reconciled
____ recorded
____ recruited
____ remodeled
____ repaired
____ reported
____ researched
____ reviewed
____ revised
____ scheduled
____ screened
____ selected
____ set up
____ simplified
____ sold
____ solved
____ strengthened
____ summarized
____ supervised
____ surveyed
____ systematized
____ taught
____ tested
____ trained
____ transformed
____ updated
____ wrote

Action Sheet 8: Action Verbs on the Job

Use the information you gathered on Action Sheet 7 to rewrite your job descriptions using action verbs. For each job you have held, choose at least three action verbs that apply to the job. Write these verbs in the column headed "Action Verb." In the next column, write the object of the verb. For example, if you wrote "simplified" in the first column, you might write "office filing system" in the second column. In the last column, write down the result of your action. If your simplification of the filing system resulted in 20 percent greater efficiency, put that in the Result column.

Position Title	Action Verb	Object	Result
Position Title	**Action Verb**	**Object**	**Result**
Position Title	**Action Verb**	**Object**	**Result**
Position Title	**Action Verb**	**Object**	**Result**

First Draft of Your Résumé

Now that you have all the information you need, you're ready to write a first draft of your résumé. Remember, you are depending on your résumé to get you an interview. To do that, it needs to be strong and concise. Your résumé is a written snapshot of your life in school and on the job. Make sure it presents you in an attractive—but honest—light.

Use short phrases that are easy to read and understand. Use action verbs to describe specific accomplishments. Avoid codes, abbreviations, and jargon unless you know the reader will know those terms.

Once the first draft is done, enter the résumé into the computer and print it out. Read it over carefully. You will probably see things you want to change. Keep working on it until you are happy with every line.

Formatting Your Résumé

The content of your résumé isn't the only part that has to be perfect. The presentation has to be good, too. Employers don't spend long reading a résumé; the average time is just 30 seconds! To make sure your résumé doesn't go straight to the "reject" pile, make it easy for an employer to read.

- Your résumé should be one page long, no longer.
- Use a computer and good-quality laser printer. (If you don't have easy access to a computer and printer, find out where you can rent time on a computer. Many copy shops have computers available this way.)
- Print it on good-quality white or cream bond paper. You may think that printing your résumé on colored paper would be a good way to make it stand out from the others, but the résumé is most readable when it is printed in black ink on white paper.
- Leave a one-inch margin on all four sides of the paper.
- Use a heading at the beginning of each section. Set the heading off by using a larger typeface or typing it in all capital letters.
- Leave a double space between sections, so that each section is clearly separated from the others.
- Don't get carried away with different typestyles; use no more than two typestyles in all.

Now start writing your résumé in the form and on the paper you will use. Show it to two or three people who know you well, and ask them for their input. You will get all kinds of ideas, good ones and bad ones, and some that contradict each other. In the end, you have to follow your own judgment.

Keep in mind that a résumé is good if it appeals to the person who reads it. And as these will be different people, they will like different things. You can never have a résumé that appeals to everybody, to all your friends, and to all the human resources people and managers who see it.

Do not go to a service that promises to create the perfect résumé for you. The résumé must reflect your personality, and therefore must be written by you, or there may be a clash between your résumé and the impression you make at the interview. That will not help you get a job!

✔ Checklist 2: Résumé Critique

Use this checklist to critique your résumé.

Overall Appearance

_____ Is the layout pleasing to look at?
_____ Is the résumé one page long?
_____ Does the résumé fit comfortably on the page?
_____ Have you used no more than two typefaces?
_____ Have you used a little bold and italic type to add interest?
_____ Are your name and phone number easily visible at the top of the page?
_____ Is the résumé on good-quality white or off-white bond paper?

Spelling

_____ Did you proofread the résumé carefully?
_____ Did you have someone else proofread your résumé?
_____ Did you use a dictionary as you wrote?
_____ Did you use the computer's spell check on the finished résumé?
_____ Did you check to make sure you didn't misuse a word, like "form" instead of "from"?

Grammar and Punctuation

_____ Did you use verb tenses consistently, with the past tense for things you did in the past, and the present tense for things you do now?
_____ Did you put a period at the end of every complete sentence?
_____ Did you capitalize all proper nouns?

Word Choice

_____ Did you use action verbs to describe your work experience?
_____ Did you check for easily confused words, like accept/except, affect/effect, personal/personnel, principal/principle?

Fact Checking

_____ Did you check that the dates of previous jobs are correct?
_____ Are your address and phone number correct?

Scannable Résumés

We saw earlier that some companies now use a computer for the first review of résumés. To make sure your résumé doesn't just get lost in the system, make sure that you include the kind of words that a computer may search for—called "keywords." Every job will have different keywords, but here are some examples:

accounting	flexible	public speaking
administration	follow-through	results-oriented
analyzed	imaginative	saved
budgeted	invented	self-starter
communication skills	leadership	sold
cost control	negotiated	takes initiative
creative	prioritized	team builder

The other important thing to remember about scanned résumés is that scanners don't "see" as clearly as human eyes do. They can confuse one character for another if the type is not clear. To make sure your résumé scans well, keep these tips in mind:

- Use a sans serif font in 11- or 12-point type. Serifs—the little "feet" on letters—can confuse a scanner. Type that is smaller than 11 points tends to look squeezed together to a scanner, while type that is too big tends to run together and blur.
- Avoid large blocks of script, italic, and underlined text.
- Don't use graphics or shading.
- Do not fold your résumé. Send it in a flat envelope. If the résumé is folded along a line of type, the scanner may find it hard to read.

Electronic Résumés

Another recent development is the electronic résumé. This is a résumé that is posted on the Internet. A number of groups and companies have developed electronic résumé databases. You can enter your résumé into one of these databases. Employers looking for people then scan the databases, again looking for keywords. Some of these sites are free; some charge a fee. There are résumé sites run by companies looking for employees, sites run by employment agencies, sites run by professional associations, and many more. Some browsers offer a listing of résumé sites, but in others you'll need to do a search. Try search terms like "job search" or "résumé database." Many sites will lead you through the process to post an on-line résumé.

When you prepare an electronic résumé, follow all the tips given above for scannable résumés. And keep these tips in mind, too:

- Avoid tabs.
- Avoid hard returns whenever possible.
- Left-justify the entire document.

PART 3

The Four Proven Ways to Find a Job

Now that you have decided what job you want and written your résumé, you are ready to start actively looking for a job.

The Public Job Market and the Hidden Job Market

The job market can be broken down in two major areas: the public job market and the hidden job market.

The public job market consists of the jobs that are offered to everybody who is interested, be it through ads in newspaper or magazines, by employment agencies or executive search companies, or over the Internet. Many people will apply for each of these open jobs, and there is a lot of competition.

The hidden job market consists of all the jobs that are filled without being offered to the public; this includes *at least half* of all jobs filled. How are they filled? Internally (within the company), through the employer's network, through recommendations, or by coincidence. In this section, you will learn how to find the hidden jobs.

What Works Best?

There are basically four ways to find a position. Everybody thinks first about answering ads in the newspaper, and then about contacting employment agencies or executive search companies. This is the public job market.

There are two other ways: sending target letters to companies that might have an interest in you, and networking—using your circle of acquaintances. This means going after the hidden job market. *More than three quarters of all jobs are found in the hidden job market.*

Let us have a good look at each of the four avenues, starting with the most successful one.

Networking

This is how 70 percent of all job seekers find a position. It is also the most difficult activity to start with, but the easiest to carry out once you are on your way.

What is networking? It is simply making use of your "network" of people you know privately or professionally. Remember, you started your networking list with Action Sheet 2.

Networking is nothing new to you; you have been doing it all your life. Maybe you asked a neighbor about a good video store, a friend about computer software, your brother about the place where he spent his last vacation, your sister about a place to buy CD's. Networking is asking people for information about something they know.

Networking is not calling all your friends, telling them that you are desperately looking for a job, and asking if they can help you. Their answer would probably be "No, I don't see how I can help you." They would be embarrassed because they do not like to say no to a friend, and you would be embarrassed because you embarrassed them.

The response would probably be different if you called and said, "Eric, you have probably heard that I just finished school. I have a plan for how to go about my job search. You have quite a bit of experience in such-and-such a field, and I would like to have your opinion about my plan and my résumé. Can we get together sometime this week for half an hour?"

Now, in this scenario, you did not ask your friend to get you a job. You asked for his advice. Eric is flattered by your confidence in his knowledge, and will go out of his way to help you. And you will get new insights, new ideas, names of companies or people to see—you can learn something from everybody!

Be sure that the person you call for a networking interview understands that you will not ask them to get you a job, that you will only ask for advice on something which that person knows better than you do.

Whom should you ask for a networking interview? Most of your relatives and friends, teachers, professors, counselors at your school, supervisors in jobs you have had, acquaintances and friends of your parents or other family members, people you know through clubs or associations—anybody who may have knowledge of the industry or the companies you are interested in, or who may know people who have such knowledge. Many of these people have spouses who work. They may have valuable connections, too!

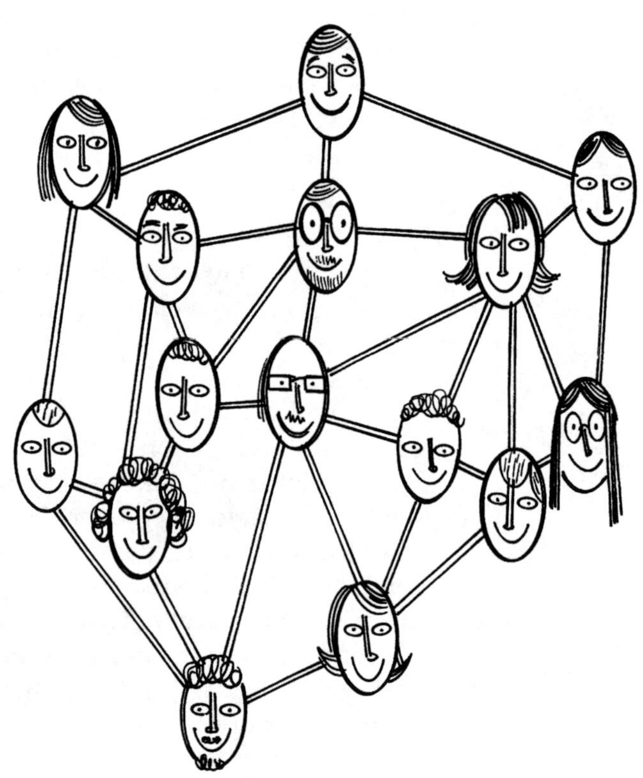

✔ Checklist 3: Networking Possibilities

- Go through your address list or address book.
- Go through your Christmas card list.
- Go through the membership list of all clubs or associations you are a member of.
- Go through the alumni list of your school or university.
- Contact your:
  - accountant
  - banker
  - businesspeople
  - Chamber of Commerce
  - classmates
  - clergy
  - dentist
  - doctor
  - former bosses
  - former colleagues
  - fraternity members
  - friends
  - insurance agent
  - lawyer
  - neighbors
  - professors
  - relatives
  - teachers

Internet discussion groups and mailing lists are another way to expand your network. These are groups of people interested in the same topic. Many mailing lists are open to the public. Some require permission to join. If you aren't already a member of an Internet discussion group, find one that interests you, and join.

Networking Interviews

The objective of a networking meeting is threefold:

- You want others to know that you are available for a job, and what kind of job you are looking for.
- You want their information and advice on some specific questions.
- You want names of people that they know who could be of help.

Before you go for a networking interview, prepare yourself.

- What information could you bring to the interview that would be of interest to your contact? This could be information about a common acquaintance, a specific company, a hobby.
- What questions do you want to ask? For example, "Here is my résumé. What do you think of it? Any suggestions for improvements?"

  "I am looking for a job (describe it). What I have planned to do is (describe it). Do you think this is a good approach?"

  "What do you think of the insurance industry, or the Globe Insurance Company? Do you know anybody in this company?"

Here is what you could say at such an interview with somebody you know (a primary contact):

> "Ed, it's good to see you. How are you?
>
> "I brought you a newspaper clipping on . . . that I thought would interest you.
>
> "Ed, as I told you, I am starting the job search process. I am not quite sure how I should go about looking for a job. I have my résumé with me. Would you mind looking at it and giving me your reaction? I have been thinking of trying in the insurance business, which you know well. Do you think that is a good idea? Can you think of any other industry I should check into? How would you go about getting into the insurance business? What insurance companies would you recommend contacting? Do you know any contact person there? Can I tell them you sent me?"

A successful networking interview should give you some new ideas and at least two new contacts for further networking interviews. When you call these secondary networking contacts, be sure to start your phone call the right way, mentioning the name of your source.

> "Mr. Prospect, my name is . . . . Our common friend Anya Meyers recommended that I call you. I just graduated from Berwick School and am looking for information about the insurance business.

You may be interrupted here as your contact says "I am very sorry, but we do not have any job openings at this moment."

Your answer should be, "Mr. Prospect, I am not looking for a job in your company at the present time. I am trying to find information and learn as much as I can about the insurance industry. Our mutual friend Ms. Meyers told me that you know the industry very well. Would you give me some of your time, about 20 minutes? Would the end of this week be convenient for you, say Thursday or Friday?"

After the networking interview, be sure to take notes, create a file card for the person interviewed (see Sample Document 10), and write a thank you letter.

Sending Target Letters

Sending out target letters is an interesting technique. On Action Sheet 2 you developed a Target List, a list of companies you thought might be interested in what you have to offer.

You will now approach these companies, but not in the usual way through their Human Resources Department. Let me explain why not.

All job openings have the same cause: a manager has a problem. When an employee leaves, the manager's problem is finding someone else to do the job. The same thing happens when an employee is promoted, or retires. The job still needs to be done. The manager has a similar problem when a new task or project is introduced: Who can do the job?

Once the manager decides to hire someone, he or she needs to get approval from a superior. Then the decision needs to be checked against the departments's budget. Next the manager tells the Human Resources Department that a new employee is needed.

If the job is a new one, the HR (Human Resources) person needs to create a job description. If the job already exists the job description needs to be reviewed.

Once the job description has been finalized, the search begins. Many companies have a rule that says they must search within the company first. If nobody suitable is found, the outside search begins. An ad is placed in the newspaper, or an employment agency is told about the job.

Next, résumés are reviewed and interviews are scheduled. Finally, one person is offered the job.

Depending on the size and complexity of the company and the urgency of the need, weeks—even months—may go by between the problem and the outside search. Human Resources will only hear about the need in halfway through the process.

If, in the meantime, you can get to the person who has the problem, telling him or her what you can do and that you are looking for a job, this person may see you as a possible solution and go directly to an interview.

This approach has two other advantages. First, you do not have a lot of competition; you may even be the only candidate. Second, the job description is not yet firmly determined, and the job may be molded around you. If you wait for step 8, you have to fit into a predetermined mold.

Of course, your target letters have much better chances of success if you have something specific to offer, something everybody else does not have.

The biggest challenge here is finding a manager with a problem you can solve. The best approach is through networking. Talk to your network. Do any of them know of an upcoming new development? This may create new jobs. An upcoming retirement, promotion, or departure may leave a position open.

The second approach calls for making an organized effort. Go back to the target list you developed in Part 1. If you have thought of more possible target companies, add them now.

Next, start phoning the companies on your list. Ask for the name of the person in charge of the department where you would like to work. Don't say that you are calling about a job, or you will be transferred to the Human Resources Department. You can say—quite tactfully—that you want to send a letter to the department head. Ask for the person's name, title, and mailing address. If you are unsure about how the manager's name is spelled, ask for that, too. Now you write your letter—*always* to a manager in charge!

Do not enclose your résumé with these letters. If a résumé is included, the letter may be directed to the Human Resources Department. Only a short letter has a chance to reach the target person, and be read.

Here is an example of such a letter.

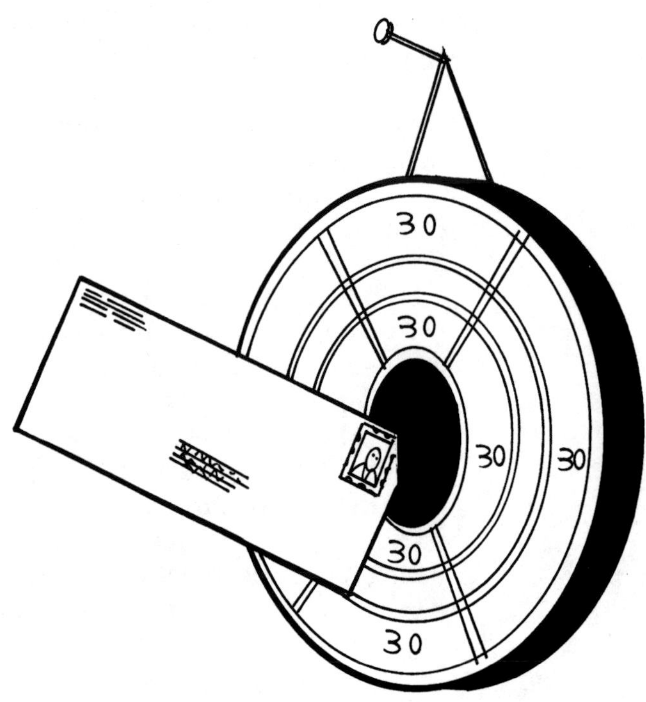

Sample Document 6: Target Letter

Jonah Ruskin
19 Novella Road
Lake Placid, NY 12845
(518) 567-8990

June 13, 1999

Mr. Jack Smith
Vice President, Production
Fine Electronics Inc.
P.O. Box 1122
Tupper Lake, NY 12433

Dear Mr. Smith:

I am a recent graduate in computer sciences from SUNY Institute of Technology, but I already have quite a bit of experience in solving practical business problems.

While in college, I worked as assistant to Professor Smolensky, and gave evening computer classes to adults. In addition, I had demanding summer jobs as programmer and analyst with an insurance company, a bank, and the FBI.

Some of my recent accomplishments include:

- Led a team of four programmers on a highly confidential project that we terminated in record time
- Was instrumental, under head coach Joe Dillinger, in rebuilding a coherent and very successful basketball team at SUNY Institute of Technology
- Improved the communication gap at Manhattan Life Insurance between the Boston office and its French-speaking Canadian subsidiary
- Created a PC-based home-schooling course based on Professor Smolensky's seminars

I would appreciate discussing the contributions I could make to your operation, and will give you a call next week to arrange a meeting.

Sincerely yours,

Jonah Ruskin

Jonah Ruskin

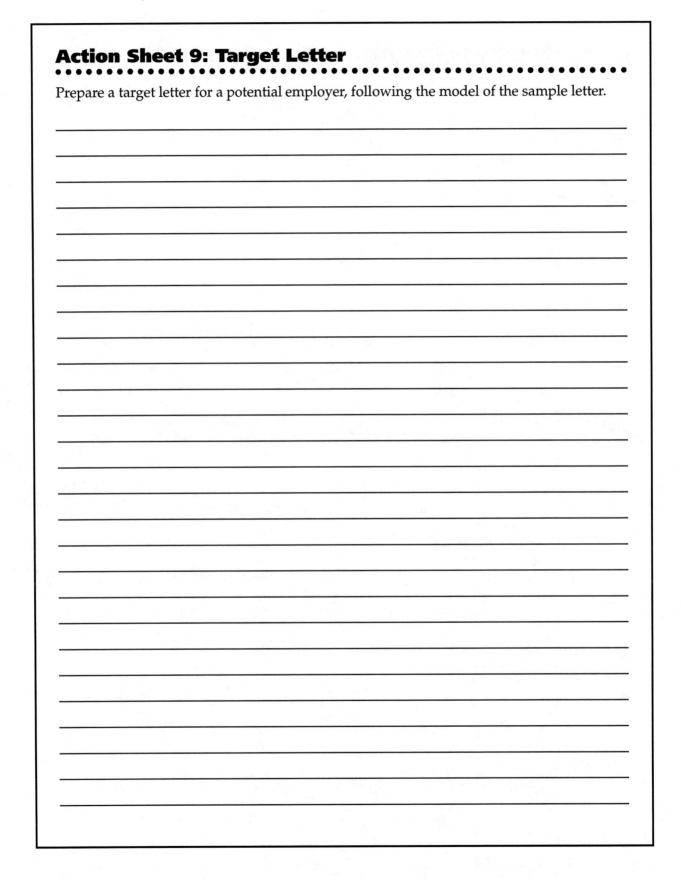

Action Sheet 9: Target Letter

Prepare a target letter for a potential employer, following the model of the sample letter.

Your Target Letter

This is a very important letter, because you will send the same letter to a number of different companies. Take two or three days, improving the letter until you are satisfied that this is the best letter you can create.

Send out your target letters, but no more than 10 or 15 a week, because of the necessary follow-up. Remember, these letters do not go to a company, they go to a person. So five to seven days after having sent the letter, you call this person on the phone, as you indicated in your letter.

Making a Follow-up Call

Often when a manager in a company reads a letter, he or she is interested, but does not have the time just now to call you. The letter gets set aside, to be acted on at a later, more convenient time.

You know what happens when you say "I can't do it now, I'll do it later." Often you don't do it at all. The same thing happens to everybody. But if the manager was interested, and you call her two or three days after she read your letter, she will be very happy to talk to you. She may even give you an interview.

Target Letter Success Rate

What success rate can you expect? A success is if you are asked to submit a résumé or—even better—are invited for an interview. If your target list was good, if you got the right names with your phone calls, and if your letter was reasonably good, you will have one success for every 10 to 15 letters you sent out, provided you follow up by phone.

So send 10 to 15 letters every week, follow up by phone, and you will have one chance a week!

Search Firms and Employment Agencies

This is the second-best way to get employed, provided you do it right and do not have false expectations. You must understand that these are two very different kinds of companies.

Employment agencies work on a nonexclusive basis. They are only paid when somebody they proposed is hired. Different employment agencies may work for the same company and on the same opening. When you give the agency your résumé, they will compare it with the open jobs they have on file, and contact you if there is a match.

Search firms or executive search firms (sometimes called "head hunters") work on an exclusive basis. They usually only work for positions that pay at least $50,000. If you are not in this league, executive search firms are not for you. The way they work is that a company gives them an exclusive mandate to look for someone. The employer pays a certain amount before the search firm even starts to work.

In both cases, these companies are paid by the hiring company. They work for, and in the interest of, the hiring company. They do not work for you, and they are not interested in your personal case. They are interested in finding somebody, anybody, for a specific job for their customer company. Do not think that when they receive your résumé you can sit back and wait until they find a job for you. That is not the way it works!

If you do pursue this course, get in touch with some good companies. Send them your résumé and call them a couple of days later and ask if they have all the information they need, or if you can help them with anything else. Also ask them if they see a good opportunity for you. Then forget about it. If they have an interesting job, they will be in touch with you. You may call back once a month, but some of them get irritated by this.

Contacting Search Firms

How do you make contact with them? You write them a letter similar to your target letter. There are two major differences: Because this is not a specific company, you have to tell them where you would like to work, and you have to include your résumé.

How do you find the companies you should write to? Employment agencies usually have ads in the newspapers, so look at the ads. If you see a specific job, refer to it; if not, just send them a general letter. You can also look at the Yellow Pages under "Employment Agencies."

Search firms do not advertise; they work only through their network. You will have to find them through the Yellow Pages under "Executive Search Firms" or through the *Directory of Executive Recruiters*, available in many libraries.

Action Sheet 10: Letter to a Search Company

Follow the same pattern as described for Action Sheet 9.

Answering Employment Ads

This looks like the easiest of the four ways. But if you want an interesting job, it is the least successful one. Nevertheless, you should answer every ad that comes close to your ideal job. The chances are slim, but they're there!

Many people write a cover letter that reads, "I saw your ad in the *XY Newspaper* and would like to apply for the job." This is a very unattractive letter. It is really saying, "I want you to read my résumé very carefully and figure out why I would be good for this job." This is definitely asking too much from your future employer.

I suggest that you take a highlighter, read the ad very carefully, and highlight everything the ad asks for. In the ad below the "highlighted" words are underlined, to show you how to do it.

Administrative Assistant

This is a challenging position for an ambitious professional to provide administrative assistance to the Market Administration Department.

You must have strong communication and organizational skills, as well as the ability to prioritize and schedule projects and meetings. Hands-on experience with Windows 95, copiers, and fax machines required.

Please send résumé to:
Jen Shrift, Head of Human Resources
The Fine Bank Inc.
P.O. Box 1122
Downtown, NY

I have underlined what the company wants. Now you have to tell Jen Shrift that you can deliver what she needs. This is what the cover letter is all about. General information about you is contained in the résumé and does not have to be repeated in the cover letter. The cover letter highlights your qualifications *for this specific job,* while the résumé gives general information about you.

Developing a Response

It is usually a good idea to choose the exact words that were used in the ad. The person who wrote the ad gave careful thought to how to formulate the company's needs. That person is probably pleased with the words he or she used. So give them back to the writer!

Do not be discouraged if an ad asks for five different qualifications and you have only three of them. Just as you have determined the ideal job knowing that you may have to make concessions, the company paints a picture of the ideal candidate in the ad. They may have to make concessions, too!

Your letter should be typed on good-quality white paper. A handwritten letter certainly gets attention, but is often not read, because no matter how clearly you write, handwriting is harder to read than typing.

Sample Document 7 is a cover letter in response to the ad above.

Sample Document 7: Letter Answering an Ad

Allen White
12 Sea Road
Upville, NY 10583
(914) 654-3219

Date

Ms. Jen Shrift
Head of Human Resources
The Fine Bank Inc.
P.O. Box 1122
Downtown, NY 10016

Re: Your ad: Administrative Assistant

Dear Ms. Shrift:

I am an ambitious graduate in office administration who can make a dedicated administrative assistant.

During my studies at Hopkins University I filled in as assistant to the Dean's office. I made many of his appointments, organized conferences, and prepared the visual aids he needed.

I was also secretary of the drama club, and published our monthly news bulletin.

I am familiar with Windows 95, Word for Windows, Excel, and PowerPoint, and with all commonly used office machines. I designed and conducted training programs for the use of sophisticated high-speed copiers in one of my summer jobs.

The enclosed résumé gives you more details about my background.

Looking forward to hearing from you, I remain,

Sincerely yours,

Allen White

Allen White

Enclosure: Résumé

Answering an Ad

Take an ad of interest to you, mark the important demands in it, and draft a cover letter. Put it away. Look at it again the next day. Does your letter answer the company's needs? Make any changes necessary, then show it to somebody you feel can help you. Then finalize the letter, type it, and send it out. The next letters will be easier for you!

Action Sheet 11: Answering an Ad

Prepare a letter in response to a Help Wanted ad. Follow the model of the sample letter.

PART 4

Your Work Plan

You know the four proven ways to find a job. Now you have to decide where to put your priorities. I would recommend using all four ways, giving first priority to networking. The time it takes to find a job depends more on how active you are than on chance or good luck.

What results can you expect? Here are some ratios, based on long experience:

Networking meetings to new networking leads	1:2
Networking meetings to job interviews	10:1
Newspaper ads to interviews	30:1
Target letters to interviews	15:1
First interviews to second interviews	3:1
Second interviews to job offers	3:1

So, how many contacts will you have to make?

- To have a choice between two jobs, you need two job offers.
- To get two job offers, you need six second interviews (2 × 3).
- To get six second interviews, you need 18 first interviews (6 × 3).
- To get 18 first interviews you need—depending on the mix of the four ways you are using—anything from 18 × 10 = 180 first contacts to 18 × 30 = 540 first contacts. Let us settle for an average of 300 first contacts.

This is a lot of first contacts! If you were satisfied with a mundane job and minimum wage, you would not have to go through all this. But this is definitely not what you want. You will have to plan your time very carefully. If you want to find a job in 8 weeks, you will have to make 35 first contacts a week. If you are willing to wait 30 weeks, you can get away with only 10 contacts a week. Make your choice!

Weekly Work Plan

Here is a weekly work plan for an active job search, about three weeks into the job search process.

Sample Document 8: Work Plan for an Active Job Searcher

One Week's Activities

Phone calls:	for networking interviews	10
	to research companies	10
	to follow up on target letters	10
	to search companies or employment agencies	3
	Total phone calls:	**33**
Letters:	target letters	10
	in response to newspaper ads	3
	follow-ups on interviews and networking interviews	10
	Total letters:	**23**
Meetings:	networking interviews	5
	first interviews	3
	second interviews	1
	Total meetings:	**9**
	Total activities for the week:	**65**

Get Organized

During the job search process, you will make a number of contacts. Soon you will not be able to remember all the names, everything you said, and what you were told. It is important that, from the very beginning of your job search, you take notes. You can use a notebook, file cards, or your computer.

For most people, large 5 × 8" file cards are the most practical. You can take them with you and update them right after a meeting, and you can arrange them in any sequence you want: alphabetical, next action, geographical—whatever is most practical for you at any given moment. Here are two examples of file cards:

Sample Document 9: Networking File Card (Front of Card)

Name

Home address

Home phone

Title

Business address

Business phone

Fax

Remarks

Sample Document 9: Networking File Card (Back of Card)

(Under the heading "Action," use *L* for letter, *F* for Fax, *P* for phone, *V* for Visit.)

Date	Action	Summary	Next step
8/8	P	will see me	8/12, 10:15 his office
8/12	V	90 minutes, very productive	2 leads, see notes
8/13	L	write thank you letter	9/10 call him

Sample Document 10: Company File Card (Front of Card)

Company name *Decorous Decor*

Address *79 East Walnut*

Directions to find *left on Main, 3 blocks, right on E. Walnut*

Phone *(512) 739–0420*

Fax *(512) 739–0421*

Important people: Name/First name *Venise Deschenes* *Title* *Vice President, Marketing*

Main Products *Import goods from Latin America, Southeast Asia*

Annual Sales/Profit per year *$22 million*

Trends

Documents consulted *Chamber of Commerce listings, newspapers, annual report*

Remarks

Sample Document 10: Company File Card (Back of Card)

(Under the heading "Action," use *L* for letter, *F* for Fax, *P* for phone, *V* for Visit.)

Date	*Action*	*Contact*	*Summary*	*Next Action*
7/16	*P*	*Venise Deschenes*	*Willing to meet me*	*7/20, set up meeting*

The Next Step

If you have followed the advice in this book, you will soon be invited for job interviews. But do not go on a job interview unprepared. Try to learn as much about the company as possible.

An interview serves to exchange information. The company wants to know more about you, and you want to know more about the company and the job. Be prepared to answer tough questions, and be prepared to ask questions yourself, so that you have all the information you want to have when you come out of the interview.

And now, I wish you, both in your job search and on the job,

Success!

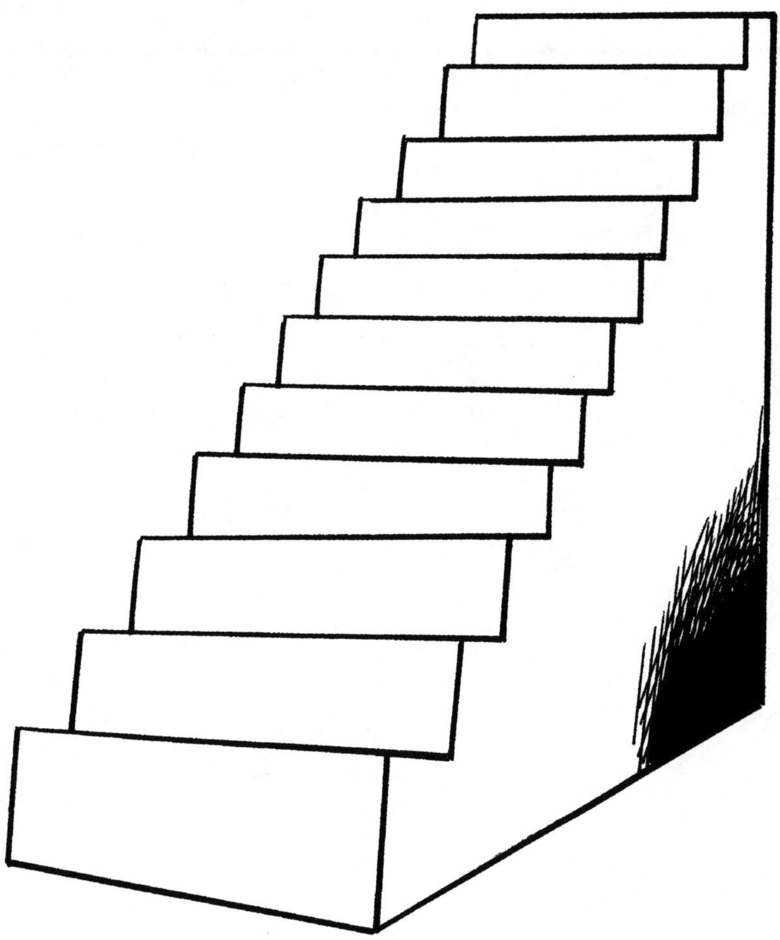